Ephemeral Tales

The Silence I Savor in Everyday Life

Janani Mohan

India | USA | UK

Made with ❤ on the BookLeaf Publishing Platform
www.bookleafpub.in
www.bookleafpub.com

Dedication

To the younger me, who dreamed without limits. Thank you for your curiosity, hope, and belief that anything was possible.

To the older me, who keeps pushing forward even when the current is strong. Keep going! You're stronger than you think; every step is still part of the story.

This is for both of us, the dreamer and the fighter.

Preface

This collection of poems is born from my own journey of healing and self-discovery. It is a reflection of the questions I have asked, the emotions I have unraveled, and the moments of clarity I have found along the way. Writing has always been my way of making sense of the world, whether in the stillness of nature, the rhythmic motion of a train, or the quiet depths of my thoughts.
I wrote my first poem, *The Mango,* when I was thirteen. Though it remained unpublished, it became the spark that ignited my love for words. Over the years, my habit of capturing fleeting thoughts, once on paper, now in the notes app on my phone, has remained a constant part of my life. Each poem in this collection is a piece of that ongoing journey.
The themes woven into these verses, nature, healing, self-exploration, and the concept of soulmates, are all deeply personal to me. They represent the path of questioning, discovering, and embracing the ever-changing self.
This book is a glimpse into my mind and heart. I hope that somewhere in these words, you find something that feels familiar, something that makes you pause, something that reminds you that you are not alone.

Acknowledgements

Writing has always been a solitary journey for me, a space where I can explore my thoughts and emotions freely. But even in solitude, I have been shaped and supported by the people around me.

To my parents, thank you for always encouraging me to follow my passion. Your honest critiques have helped me refine my voice, and your unwavering support has given me the strength to keep going. No matter how deeply I retreat into my writing, I know you are always there.

To the few who have understood my quiet world and respected the space I need to create, I am grateful. Your silent support, your patience, and your belief in me mean more than words can express.

Though I write alone, this collection carries traces of those who have influenced, inspired and stood by me. For that, I am deeply thankful.

1. Pokój Pokoju

A room of peace,
Filled with the effervescences of midnight jasmines,
And a window to view the sky and beyond,
Is a place I call Home.

Morning meditation, afternoon siestas,
Enlightening evenings, magical midnights
And a music box that connects me to the world,
Is a place I call Home.

Coffee roast aroma, flavorful biryanis,
Jackfruit delicacies, mom's love,
And a garden to feel the power of the creator,
Is a place I call Home.

Lazy Ginger, my beige and white cat
Adventurous Kai, my sterling blue betta fish,
And a soulmate who owns my heart,
Is a place I call Home.

My writing desk, my rainbow lamp,
A world of memories, soft and damp,
Tiny treasures from journeys far,
Is a place I call home.

Books stacked high, with tales to share,
Coins and stamps from places rare,
Robots I build in my time to spare,
Is a place I call home.

In times of chaos and burdened hearts,
Come to the place I call home,
In search of your inner child to unveil the power within
you,
Come to the place I call home.

2. La'i

Tit tat trot, fell the acorn from the Dawn Redwood tree,
As I sat down under its shade to set my mind free,
Behold cried the Blue Jay, alerting my senses to focus,
As the Female Mallard searched for food without much
ruckus.

Persistent calls of little birds fill the air,
Reminding me of all the banters my sisters share,
The zooming airplane buzzes high up in the sky,
nudging me of adventures I ought to try.

A dragonfly drones in the nearby pond,
Its little wings carrying her far and beyond,
Teaching me a lesson to learn,
Little or big, you reach the heights you often yearn.

A little chipmunk approaches from the bushes,
Ever cautious, not to make a single sound.
Its silence reminds me of times gone by,
When I chose to observe, and not to react, but just be
found.

The rustling leaves, a soft breeze flowing by,
Reminds me of afternoon siestas, left behind,

The sounds of nature, fleeting like the day,
Ephemeral, they come, and then drift away.

Each sound, a whisper of life's passing grace,
Appearing, vanishing, in time's embrace.
I savor the moments, as they slip through my hands,
Like grains of sand, carried by unseen strands.

We emote with nature, in tune with the skies,
In the rustling, the wind, the soft sun's rise.
For every fleeting sound, a story untold,
A reminder that beauty can never grow old.

3. Tabi no Iyashi

Scattered pieces of my shattered heart,
Calling out loud, tearing me apart.
I miss you all, but I must move on,
Some days it's easy, others it's long.

I wake to an emotional whirlpool's tide,
Some days, I lay, letting the pain collide.
Staring at the blank space above,
Where thoughts swirl, and pain creeps, unshoved.

Sparingly, I care for this hurt within,
Old friend, emotions withheld, where do I begin?
I scream inside, cry out loud,
Lost in the noise of my own cloud.

A song plays, waging a war in my mind,
Battling for space, for peace to find.
Some days it wins, bringing calm once more,
And I dance with my childhood friend on the floor.

An imaginary friend, from a time gone by,
Filling my heart, beneath the sky.
Helping the inner child feel fulfilled,
As always, in the dance, we're both healed.

4. L'Abito dei Colori

Have you wondered of the gown you wear,
A cloak of colors beyond compare?
Bestowed upon you from the start,
It's woven with the threads of your heart.

Each shade, unique, a silent light,
Shining bright when joy takes flight.
It darkens when harm is done,
A quiet witness to each undone.

But no judgment can stain its hue,
No words or thoughts can break it through.
This gown, a reflection deep within,
It speaks your truth when you're alone, unseen.

The world may offer gowns of gold,
But your true gown is yours to hold.
It doesn't fade, it doesn't fray,
It simply waits for you each day.

So will you wear it with pride, unafraid,
Or hide its colors in the shade?
It shines its brightest when you are true,
Embrace the gown that speaks of you.

5. Amore Perduto

You were my drug
You were my fallacy
You made me dream
You made me happy

You come and go
You stir my soul
You make me high
You are my dole

The rush is real
My hormones feel surreal
Adrenaline floods my veins
Spinning fantasies in my brain

Reality is an illusion
Locking me in seclusion
Reaching you is far fetched
Pain is but deeply etched

You are gone too soon
Not sure if it's a boon
I fight the demons within me
To strive to live a life in peace

Goodbye, my pain
Goodbye, my hope
Inspire me to revive my purpose
And spin magic upon this surface!

6. Chandra Baalika

Walking through the wooded forest,
I weave through trees to find my sight,
I've traveled far to meet you at your brightest light,
For I am your Moon Child.

I hear water splash nearby,
Peering through the leaves,
I glimpse the light you cast,
A memory I hold with my inner eye.

I dive deep into the cascades,
Soaking in the magic of moonlight,
My spirit is reborn,
And my inhibitions fade away.

No fear, no pain,
No burdens, no grief
For I am free to be wild,
I am your Moon Child.

7. Liten Frisk Damm

Come summer, lilies bloom,
Come autumn, dogs swim,
Come winter, kids skate,
Come spring, swans breed.
Thou art a pond for all seasons.

Meandering duck parade,
Paddling through floating lilies,
A happy duck mom teaching the ducklings,
To swim, feed and survive.
A sight to behold on a summer noon!

Buzzing dragonflies,
Raccoon crossings in twilight,
Playful dogs, and leaf transformations,
Some red, some orange and some green,
All summing up as autumn sets in!

Frigid waters covering its breadth,
Cardinal sightings in the bushes,
Ice skater twirling in the chilling wind,
Amidst magical snowflakes falling from the sky,
Winter is here, fear not.

Mating swans, baby pink cherry blossoms,
Swaying breeze, calls of Red-winged Blackbirds soaring low,
New leaves, clear waters, and Canadian geese,
A soothing sunshine blushing in,
All welcome Spring together at the fresh pond.

8. Maladie

There is an explosion, a deep ache,
A harbinger of greater misfortune,
The fort trembles with its vibration,
The fort that guards the human soul.

The explosion echoes through the chambers,
In the deepest heart of the fort,
The guards swiftly carry the signal,
To the king who rests high above.

The king commands his army to charge,
A defensive plan is set in motion,
The movement halts, poised for the next blow,
Ready to protect the soul from the coming storm.

The explosion does not repeat,
But its impact lingers long,
External help lends a steady hand,
And soon, the peace is born.

9. Gül

The epitome of innocent love,
To your beauty, one does bow,
Your mild fragrance fills the air,
Soothing hearts with tender care.

In the nearby cottage, you bloom,
In pairs and clusters, you chase my gloom,
Tempting all who pass you by,
To envy your charm with a sigh.

You are a reflection of the life on earth,
Thorns marking internal strife and birth,
Bold flowers stand with courage bright,
Then fade away, for none escapes the night.

A petal-less rose, a mournful sight,
Like the world without its light.
Yet tender buds in shrubs await,
To bloom in full glory, opening the gate,
A hope ignites my heart anew,
That life must go on and we must too!

10. Schaduw

My lifetime companion, you are,
You travel with me near and far.
A silent message you convey to all,
That no one is lonely after all.

When the whole world considers me small,
You amplify my confidence, making me tall,
Blooming happiness in my heart,
For you are inseparable, a vital part.

The art of deciphering animals you taught,
Evolving the creativity my mind had sought,
Your existence, a constant reminder,
That light is a requirement of the living lot.

You hold more than what meets the eye,
The dark corners of my heart where I often lie,
Confronting my deepest fears within,
Is the only way to meet my truest form herein.

11. Alternatives Universum

Somewhere in an alternate universe,
We are all born with blue eyes,
With faces shaped like the moon,
Waxing out and waxing in.

As seasons change, so do our moods,
Yet we remain serene and whole.
There is peace within, peace around,
For we all share the same soul.

No noise, no fight, just silent flow,
We all work toward a shared goal,
To serve a common Master,
Who feeds us every night.

Commands are sent to our neurons,
And we all hail the Master's call,
Running off on simple errands,
With no emotions at stall.

No selfish thoughts, no bonds lost,
No betrayals, no divided cause,
For in adversity, we find it true,
In times of trial, we are one crew.

12. O que nos limita?

Life confines us,
Or rather, my mind confines me,
The life I perceive in my mind,
Holds me back, limits me.

Fear adds the restrictions,
The scar of unexpected pain,
Adds more constrictions,
To the fear of being hurt again.

Some days I feel trapped,
I wake with a clouded mind,
A heavy heart and an unsure face,
Questioning my very existence.

What drives us to form expectation
In the first place?
Why paint pictures of the future,
Why pour ink all over it?

What makes me happy, I ask,
I struggle with the answer, overthinking starts,
Losing control once again,
But wait, did I ever have control in the first place?

What is control,
Is it when RHS = LHS?
Is it when what I expect, is what happens?
Is that reality better?

They say the sky is the limit,
But I say otherwise, your mind is your limit.
Break those limiting thoughts,
Tear down the walls and all the distraught.

Battling conflicting thoughts throughout,
I journal, I pour my heart out,
I feel a little lighter somehow,
With clouds clearing, I feel warmth now.

13. Emotsiya

We label our emotions with colors and names,
Happy, sad, angry like shadows and flames,
Yet beyond these labels, what do we find?
A vast sea of feelings, all intertwined.

Shame whispers softly, disappointment sighs,
Hopelessness lingers, while the spirit denies.
Mind-blocked and tired, exhausted we call,
But there is a beauty in feeling, in embracing it all.

Butterflies flutter, lightness take flight,
Bliss in the stillness, dreams in the night.
Carefree and tender, dreamy and free,
Emotions so fleeting, yet wild as the sea.

Elation and pride, a burst of the sun,
Feeling accomplished, the race finally won.
Lazy and breezy, with moments to spare,
The weight of the world seems light in the air.

Disgust and annoyance. dismay in the breeze,
Terrified whispers, trapped with no ease.
Shocked and drained, emotionless stone,
Troubled and weighed, feeling alone.

Lonely and rejected, self-loathing deep,
Critical judgements, harsh words to keep.
Nervousness trembling, anxiety's reign,
Yet in the stillness, we are not meant to remain.

Next time you feel, don't rush to define,
Sit with the surge, let your heart realign.
Write your feeling, pour it all out,
Emotions will pass, without a need to shout.

When joy fills your soul, dance in the light,
Sing it aloud, share, and revel in delight,
When sorrow or rage swells in deep,
Release it in silence, or shed in weep.

Walk through nature, let music take hold,
Find peace in the pauses, in moments of gold.
And once the storm has cleared your mind,
Reflect and decide, with wisdom to find.
For peace is a treasure, happiness a friend,
In this fleeting life, let joy never end.

14. Havevenner

In the early dawn, a pair takes flight,
Pigeons from the east, quenching their thirst at first
sight,
The mynas arrive as the sun climbs high,
With calls that echo and fill the sky.

The myna, a messenger, with shrills so clear,
Announces a water body, drawing near,
She sips from the tub, then bathes with delight,
Flapping her wings, her joy taking flight.

The male follows, repeating the same,
Hunting for food, playing the game.
The crows arrive with "Ca Ca" calls,
Sharing our lunch, sitting on the terrace walls.

Afternoon's warmth brings a sea breeze to the land,
As we rest in peace, in slumber's hand.
Midday baths stir, waking me from my nap,
The Coucal steps in, a majestic chap.

With brown-feathered wings and blackened coat,
He drinks and strolls, on a plantain he'll gloat,
Singing his song, he leaves with grace,

My grandmother smiles at his lucky trace.

Superstitions are shared, a tale unfolds,
When a loud call of the Rufous Treepie bold,
Arrives in pairs, their cackling fight,
As they sip and nibble, in the afternoon light.

Tea time arrives with masala chai,
The family gathers to share gossip as the moments fly,
As the evening comes, the sun paints the sky,
Orange and pink, as the day waves goodbye.

Ginger the cat, in her playful reign,
Stretching and yawning, cuddled without any pain.
Naughty, yet graceful she claims her space,
In the garden, she roams, with a regal grace.

Though she resists love, we care for her still,
A bowl of milk and quiet goodwill.
Ginger, once lost, now calls this home,
In our backyard, she is never alone.

We share our lives, our hearts, and the day,
With avian friends and pets at play,
Food and water, freely given,
For nature's gifts are meant for all, unbidden.

15. Dadirri

Here I am, a child of nature's grace,
Seated on thy lap, in a quiet space,
In silence, I listen to thy soothing voice,
As the calming breeze makes my spirit rejoice.

The buzzing bees, a melody so sweet,
My lips curl upward, my heart skips a beat.
Aren't we all children, who lose their way,
Only to find peace in nature's sway?

Here I sit, seeking my heart's release,
Yearning for a moment of calm, of peace,
Where my heart is light, my mind is clear,
And I feel my inner self drawing near.

A stork upon the tree, regal and wise,
Viewing the world with knowing eyes.
Her friend, the red-winged blackbird flies,
Exchanging tales beneath the open skies.

Another bird shrieks, hidden in the flowers' embrace,
I long to see her, but find joy in her grace.
Her mystery lingers, unseen yet near,
A reminder that some things are not to appear.

I smell the color green, so pure, so bright,
The dews on the grass, the lake's quiet might,
The bark beneath my fingers, strong and old,
Holds memories of lives, young and bold.

Away from the noise, from worry and strife,
In thy company, I find the rhyme of life,
No masks to wear, no burdens to bear,
Just nature's warmth, free from despair.

In silence, I speak, in silence, I see,
For thou art my oldest friend, Mother Nature, to me.
I belong to thee, in thy arms, I find rest,
For with thee, my soul is always blessed.

16. Peojeul Hateu

Our heart, a puzzle, empty and wide,
A space for pieces, scattered outside.
Each piece is unique, intricately shaped and true,
A lesson, an experience, meant just for you.

As life unfolds, we gather them near,
Each jagged edge, each corner, each sphere.
We place them carefully, one by one,
Filling the jigsaw, until it's complete.

Some pieces may slip, some may be lost,
Distracted by the world, we pay the cost.
But in the end, there is no repent,
For each of us leave with a full heart.

What once was hollow, dark, and cold,
Transforms to peace, vibrant and bold.
The puzzle finished, everything fits in,
A perfect picture, a peaceful red glow.

17. Ki vagyok?

I see the shift within,
A change so subtle, yet profound,
But who am I beneath the skin?
What's the peace I seek to find, where's it found?

The mind, a restless river, churns,
Its current pulls, yet to know,
The answers that the heart still yearns,
As time moves on, too fast to show.

The world, oblivious, marches on,
Its steps are heavy, slow and blind,
While questions whisper in the dawn,
And leave their mark upon the mind.

Why am I made for such a fight?
A struggle with a self that cries,
The soul, a wanderer in the night,
Seeking truth beneath the skies.

I crave the days when time would smile,
When faces met, and hearts would speak,
Where laughter dances in the open aisle,
And life was pure, not fake or weak.

Can we return to those soft winds,
When hearts would meet with ease?
When the world wasn't ruled by digital sins,
And moments bloomed, too fast to pass?

Yet here I stand, with questions wide,
The answers like the stars, far yet bright,
I chase them through the changing tide,
With a hope to greet my happy soul in sight.

18. Jaan

Swans glide through the silent sky,
Bound to one, they soar high,
A symbol of love that will never fade,
Two souls bound, their path beautifully laid.

But what if this tale is just a dream,
A myth spun from man's restless scheme?
What if the heart, in its endless chase,
Has simply invented a longing, a place?

We search for a connection, a spark, a sign,
A destiny, that you will be mine.
What happens when the dream fades gray,
And the one you sought slips away?

Do our minds weave fantasies, unreal?
What is this force, this magnetic feel?
The hormones that dance, the emotions that sway,
What does it mean when we yearn for a play?

The questions arise, too many to name,
Each one a spark, each one a flame.
We meet broken souls, each scarred by the past,
Yet healing their wounds, learning to last.

I, too, am wounded, but healing inside,
My heart grows stronger with each tear I hide,
The road to recovery, though long and steep,
Has taught me to rise and not fall too deep.

Shortcomings will come, disappointments will stay,
But hope for the future that lights my way.
So let go of the pain, let go of the fear,
And trust that the best is always near.

For soulmates aren't made, they are found to heal,
Two broken souls, learning to feel.
Not perfect, not flawless, but ready to rise,
Together, as swans, beneath endless skies.

19. Mosaik av själar

In every word, in every glance,
We leave behind a fleeting dance,
A piece of us, a little thread,
Woven through the paths we have tread.

When I look at the way I move, the way I stand,
I find pieces of others, like water droplets on the sand,
How I bid goodbye, with a stylish wave,
A gesture learned from a friend so brave.

The way I hold hands, with a tender might,
A borrowed warmth from someone who made me bright.
How my braid falls, neatly tied,
A memory of a love I could never hide.

Each little thing, each quiet trace,
A complex theme in life's pace,
We are ever-changing, yet somehow the same,
A blend of voices, a silent flame.

So shine, dear soul, in your quiet way,
For you carve your light in each new day.
Every moment, every touch, a mark so deep,
A memory planted, a promise to keep.

We are mosaics, stitched with care,
A patchwork of love that we receive and share,
Each heartbeat, each laugh, each tender sigh,
Etches a story that will never die.

20. Amigos perdidos

On a Friday morn, I dreamt in fright,
Of friends now gone, lost from my sight.
I miss them so, their laughter and cheer,
A bond once close, now distant, unclear.

Some drifted away, and others I let go,
Yet memories linger, and time does flow.
We sat beneath that tree, and laughed on that wall,
Sharing moments so pure, I recall it all.

Birthdays celebrated, icecream to share,
Those moments of joy, beyond compare,
I wish I could meet them, as they once were,
To relive the past, with hearts full of care.

But change has arrived, for them and for me,
We have both grown and shifted, as life does decree.
Yet in that snapshot, love still resides,
In the laughter, the banter, where joy never hides.

For maybe that's all we can do,
Love them in the moment, when they were true,
Because life moves on, and time doesn't wait,
You can't go back, no matter your state.

So live every moment, with all your might,
For you can't relive what fades into night.
Cherish today, as if it's the last,
For once it's gone, it's gone too fast.

21. Homecoming

Across the globe miles away
Lies my throbbing heart
For that's where my family stay
Ambition separating us apart!

Each day goes by with a call
Sharing brunt, tears and smiles
I await the day my semester ends
For off I fly without a stall!

Five months pass by in a whiff
I wonder how I survived this trip
I now say with a sigh of relief
I am all set for my home-bound trip!

The day of the journey arrives
I bid goodbye to the snow and ice
My mind tunes to the waves of my town
And the sea breeze fills my soul with warmth and love!